Alain deGlanv

PASSWORD

MAGIC

IS THE *ULTIMATE SOLUTION* TO THE

GREAT PASSWORD DILEMMA!

AT LAST, CREATING SECURE, UNBREAKABLE PASSWORDS,
ACTUALLY WRITING THEM DOWN IN A LIST THAT NO ONE BUT
YOU CAN UNDERSTAND, AND EASILY REMEMBERING HOW TO
ENTER THESE "GIBBERISH" PASSWORDS WHEN LOGGING IN IS

AS EASY AS

ONE – TWO – THREE!!

HOW TO CREATE AND REMEMBER HIGHLY SECURE PASSWORDS

as many as you want - and it's as EASY AS 1 - 2 - 3!

ESCAPE THE MADNESS! Finally, an END to the Great PASSWORD DILEMMA. Here is a system you can use to create excellent, highly secure passwords (a different one for each account,) and then actually write them down on paper for all to see in a manner only you can understand.

More importantly, even others who've read this book shall find themselves completely frustrated should they attempt to read your list.

No software to buy, no additional equipment, no Memory Tricks. Everything you need is in this book (except for your notebook and pencil.)

AND IT'S FUN!

Alain deGlanville developed The Alain Code system over a period of seven years after finding himself ever more frustrated by the RULES of SECURE PASSWORDS: Never use names of people, places, etc.; no phone numbers, addresses, birthdates... DO USE nonsense sequences of letters, numbers and symbols, and NEVER WRITE THEM DOWN!

IMPOSSIBLE!?!

Not for Alain, and now, *NOT FOR YOU!*

Alain deGlanville's

PASSWORD

MAGIC

THE ULTIMATE SOLUTION TO THE

GREAT PASSWORD DILEMMA!

Password Magic

Table of Contents

Alain deGlanville's

PASSWORD

MAGIC

THE ULTIMATE SOLUTION TO THE

GREAT PASSWORD DILEMMA!

Copyright

Foreword

This project has been developing itself over the past few years as I found myself in need of ever more numerous passwords, in an increasingly internet-dominated world; and found myself confronted by the same obstacles facing most internet users – the management of those passwords, and the rules that create the *GREAT PASSWORD DILEMMA...*

1. <u>DO</u> <u>NOT</u> USE *common words or numbers*
    a. NO NAMES of family, friends, pets, places, foods, films, actors, politicians, cars, sports, teams, streets, cities, books, and so on...
    b. NO BIRTHDATES, phone numbers, addresses, zip codes, driver's licenses, anniversaries, ages, or other numbers that may have any significance to me personally.
2. <u>DO</u> use *nonsensical sequences* of letters and numbers
    a. Use both *upper* and *lower case* letters
    b. Use *punctuation* and other *symbols* where permitted
    c. UNPRONOUNCEABLE and unmemorizable Passwords are best
3. USE <u>DIFFERENT</u> Passwords for each account

4. <u>NEVER</u> WRITE passwords down *anywhere*

Impossible!

How is one to observe all of the above without becoming a lunatic? Imagine a password like "eT6_8!y7S" and trying to memorize it. In fact, imagine a list of a half-dozen such maddening creations and memorizing *all* of them, *and* remembering which one belongs to which account! It's possible, I suppose, that one person in a billion possesses the magical mind needed for such a task, but that certainly doesn't include me, nor the bulk of humanity, I'm certain.

So for those of us attempting to function normally in the regular world, it's a problem, isn't it? I know you've faced this dilemma, and, as I have, you've most likely broken – nay, *destroyed* – most of the above rules. And while it has made the handling of passwords generally easier, it has also compromised the security of our personal information to an astounding degree.

PROBLEM SOLVED! Finally there is a system everyone can use to create excellent, highly secure passwords, a different one for each account, and then actually write them down on paper for all to see in a manner only the owner of the list can understand!

More importantly, even others who've read this book and learned the system shall find themselves properly stymied should they attempt to read your list.

For example, if I were to post a password list on my computer or desk like the one on the next page, you'd think I'd gone round the bend…

ACCOUNT	*PASSWORD*
Internet Logon	Le2)32^w4
Bank Online	yw1-82*B27r2!
Computer Logon, office	!b2Z-84*

However, let anyone attempt to *use* any of those "passwords," and *they'll* be the ones going berserk! While *I* on the other hand, can glance at my list and instantly key in the appropriate *password*.

Magic?

YES!

But is every potential thief doomed to failure? Let's be realistic! Out there in the world of dedicated cyber-criminals, there are those who possess the unlimited means and single-mindedness of ill purpose necessary to wreak havoc upon the unsuspecting. They have on their hard drives the latest versions of the latest releases of the latest software developed for the purpose of constructing every possible combination of letters, numbers and symbols in the known universe! They have hacked their way through the most "secure" networks out there, seeped through miniscule cracks in the thickest firewalls, and slithered into the myriad mazes of the most encrypted files of governments and corporations alike. They know no shame, and have no other life (which is fortunate, as the likelihood they'll reproduce is remote.)

The good news is that such incidents are diminishing in volume. Business globally has strengthened its security, and even governments, normally slow to pick up on good ideas, are following suit. Operating systems are shipping with software-based *firewall* protection built in, and many internet service providers are offering free virus protection to email clients.

Even so, you and I must be vigilant! We must never assume that we are safe; and this is most important- we must accept full responsibility for our own personal security. This is why I've created *Password Magic.*

Most home users of computers don't have quite the security problems of businesses, governments and major corporations. Specifically, password thieves would be more interested in getting into a bank database than your private email. Your personal passwords would not likely command the same high price at market as perhaps the password your neighbor uses to log on to his computer at the I.R.S. Therefore the rules for creating secure passwords are slightly more relaxed when it comes to those we use at home to retrieve email, and conduct personal business on the internet.

Not that we should relax altogether. Never! But if we were to look at password security as having *levels*, our personal home passwords might be at only Level 1, while we may require a Level 2 or Level 3 password at work. (For perspective, most passwords in use around the world today are so *in*secure, I would place them at a Level *"minus 3!"* To advance even to Level 1 should increase general security exponentially a hundred-fold!)

Now, as you might guess, creating a Level 1 password is significantly easier than creating a Level 3. And as most computer users will never require anything over a Level 1 or 2, it seemed a waste of time and effort to delve that deeply into the subject.

This book teaches the entire philosophy and concept of the *Alain Code System,* covered here in Chapters 1 through 6, where you shall discover the secrets to a solid set of Level 1 Passwords.

In the later Chapters, we shall explore bringing your Passwords up to Level 2, or even Level 3 as you choose.

Lastly, a word about the name – *The Alain Code*. It's vanity, of course. You'll forgive, I trust, a gentleman's fantasy of living to hear people speaking of "The Alain Code," as the term worms its way into the lexicon.

And if it doesn't – oh well…

Alain deGlanville, July 17, 2010

Alain deGlanville

Chapter One

OVERVIEW

(Prepare Yourself...)

> **CAUTION:**
> *SKIMMING THROUGH THIS BOOK BEFORE OFFICIALLY BEGINNING CAN BE DANGEROUS! YOU'LL NOTICE SOME RATHER FRIGHTENING DIAGRAMS, SYMBOLS, AND OTHER NOTATIONS THAT ON FIRST GLANCE MAY APPEAR IMPOSSIBLY COMPLEX.*
>
> *BE ASSURED HOWEVER, THAT IT'S ALL QUITE SIMPLE. EVERYTHING IS LAID OUT IN AN EASY, STEP-BY-STEP LESSON FORMAT AND YOU MAY PROCEED WITHOUT FEAR! JUST DON'T SCARE YOURSELF TO DEATH IN PREVIEWS...*

YOU ARE ABOUT TO LEARN the *Alain Code System*, how it works and how to use it. You are about to discover how incredibly simple and easy it is to create and maintain a long list of highly secure Passwords that you'll never have to remember! You are about to find that you really can follow all the most stringent rules of password security, and do so with no effort at all.

There are three steps to the System:

1. **Forge Your Keys**

    a. The foundation of your personal Password System is made up of your personal *Password Keys*

2. **Create Your Passwords**

    a. Using your personal *Keys*, you shall build a list of unique Passwords, quickly and easily

3. **Lock Your Passwords (*Encoding*)**

    a. Using the copyrighted *Alain Code*, you will create a list of coded, easy instructions that you alone can understand.

It's true. Even others who've read this book and learned the System shall be unable to decipher your list! Step three is what actually makes it all possible. Using the *Alain Code*, you'll create easy instructions for each Password on your list. The instructions are simple and easy to read, and allow you to convert them into any Password on your list with remarkable speed.

Three easy Steps – *As easy as 1 – 2 – 3!*

Alright, yes – it does involve some work on your part to *learn* the *System*. It's not difficult, and there are a few exercises and practices to help you learn. The only materials you'll need are this book, a notebook and pen or pencil.

An important note regarding security: You'll want access to a paper shredder of the *cross-cut* style. Do not make notes in this book! You should keep all of your notes and exercises in your special notebook, and after you finish the lessons you'll remove all your pages of notes and exercises and commit them to the shredder.

If you do not have your own personal vault, a fully secure safe to which no one else has access, then I urge you to rent a safe deposit box at your bank. It should be your box and yours alone, not shared with anyone. Upon finishing this book, there is something you'll want to lock in it if you haven't a vault. (In fact, in many ways a bank safe deposit box is more secure than a home safe.)

Password Security is quite a serious matter, but that doesn't mean it has to be difficult. I created this *System* out of necessity, primarily because I'm lazy and wanted it all to be easy. And I succeeded. I'm rather proud of *The Alain Code* (as evidenced by its name,) and I know you'll find it's just what you've been seeking. But be very good to yourself and *do the exercises!* They are vital to the learning process, and they're not difficult.

And simply because it's a serious subject, doesn't mean it must be dull. So be prepared to enjoy the journey…

Alain deGlanville

Chapter Two

PART ONE – Three Steps

STEP ONE: Create Your KEYS; the *Keyword*

(Your KEYS to Success...)

A: Overview

          IN THE NEXT TWO Chapters, you'll learn how to create your own personal *Keys*.

You may be wondering why I'm using the plural form of *Key*. Just how many of these things must one create and remember? Happily, the answer is *only two*. That's all. You shall create both a *Key Word* and a *Key Number*. And you'll see how simple the process is, and how easy it'll be to remember them.

Now if you've read any guidelines to good passwords, you'll be familiar with the *rules*:

1. **DO NOT USE** *common words or numbers*

    a. **NO NAMES of family, friends, pets, places, foods, films, actors, politicians, cars, sports, teams, streets, cities, books, and so on...**

    b. **NO BIRTHDATES, phone numbers, addresses, zip codes, driver's licenses, anniversaries, ages, or other numbers that may have any significance to you personally.**

2. **_DO_ use _nonsensical sequences_ of letters and numbers**
    a. **Use both _upper_ and _lower case_ letters**
    b. **Use _punctuation_ and other _symbols_ where permitted**
    c. **UNPRONOUNCEABLE and unmemorizable Passwords are best**

3. **USE DIFFERENT Passwords for each account**
4. **NEVER WRITE passwords down _anywhere_**

Good Grief! How is one to follow all of those? Relax. In a short time you'll have all the answers. But first, let's look quickly at the logic behind these rules.

Number 1 above is simple to understand. If you were to use a name, number or phrase that is well known to you, others – particularly those who know you – would have a good shot at guessing it. Yet people violate this rule all the time, simply because they want passwords that are easy to remember!

Number 2 is of great import. A "nonsense" _sequence_ of characters is virtually impossible to guess or figure out, simply because it makes no sense whatever. Why don't most people use them? As _nonsense sequences_ are nearly impossible to memorize,

> ## Sequence:
>
> *The progression (normally from left to right) of any given unified grouping of Characters recognized as either a whole word or number, or a given Segment of either.*

people are forced to write them down – a truly awful idea! So one has the choice of violating either Rule #2 or Rule #4.

And if someone were to discover a Password, and the same one had been used for all one's accounts, guess what? Disaster! (Rule #3...)

Now here's the good news: There's a simple, easy way to overcome *all* of these concerns, and it's as easy as *1 – 2 – 3*.

B: The Keyword

The *Keyword* has three major characteristics:

1. 2 or 3 syllables of nonsense
2. No repeating characters
3. Pronounceable and memorizable

(A note on Number 3- even though the **passwords** created from the *Keyword* shouldn't be pronounceable, the *Keyword* itself <u>must</u> be.)

And a quick word regarding non-alpha Symbols ($ # & * ^, etc.): While there are online providers that allow the use of symbols as part of one's password, there are many that do not. Therefore, the early chapters of this book are devoted to creating a core Password System (*The Alain Code System*) without the use of such symbols. These Passwords are referred to as *Core* Passwords.

Alain deGlanville

(In later chapters, we'll deal with these *symbols*.)

There are two methods of creating the *Keyword*. I'll teach you both of them, then let you decide which to use. Before the end of this Chapter, you'll have created your own personal *Keyword* that you shall use for many years, so don't be afraid to try both methods, coming up with 2 or 3 *Keywords* from which to make a selection.

The two methods are quite simply the *Short Phrase* and the *Long Phrase* methods.

C: SHORT PHRASE METHOD

This method asks you to scare up a two-word phrase for raw material. Now, it's most important that the phrase be something that no one should ever associate with you. As an example, if someone who knew me well were to try to guess some phrases for which I might have a fondness, or that might have some special significance to me, "golf cart" wouldn't even be on the list. Never in my life have I expressed or shown any interest in the sport. I don't follow it on television, don't discuss it with friends, and know fellows like Arnold Palmer and Tiger Woods only from their television appearances.

(Now that I've offended the golfers among you – it's not personal really, I simply never caught the bug – we may continue.) The point is that "golf cart" is a perfectly acceptable phrase for me, while it might be an utterly disastrous choice for the aforementioned Mr. Palmer.

"golf cart"

I shall now manipulate this phrase in *three ways*.

1. Sequence Inversion
2. Syllable Inversion (optional)
3. Case

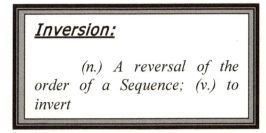

Inversion:

(n.) A reversal of the order of a Sequence; (v.) to invert

The "Sequence" is the string of characters (alphabet letters.) That is, "golfcart." Inversion means to reverse the sequence: "tracflog" – simply spelled backwards!

The optional syllable inversion requires first breaking this new nonsense word into its syllables, "trac" and "flog," and then reversing them, "flog – trac."

Now we have, "flogtrac."

You may or may not choose to invert your syllables – that's up to you. I chose to do so in this case because "flogtrac" seems a bit more fun to pronounce than "tracflog." Purely a personal choice of course, but remember that in the end you'll have to memorize your

Alain deGlanville

Keyword and never forget it. So why not make it something that pleases you?

Before proceeding further, let's review the rules for an acceptable Keyword:

1. 2 or 3 syllables of nonsense
2. No repeating characters
3. Pronounceable and memorizable

Does "flogtrac" fit the bill? It's two syllables, and it's nonsense, isn't it? It's not a real word, has no definition, and is not currently in use among the english-speaking peoples of this planet.

There are no repeating characters. Each letter in the word occurs only once! *f l o g t r a c*

Is it pronounceable? Yes. We can actually say the word without injuring our tongues. But what about memorizing it? Believe it or not, a silly word like this is actually easier to remember than one might think. In fact, I'll warrant you've already done so. *flogtrac*

This manipulation involves working with the individual syllables of the *Keyword*, so just a note here on **syllables**: There are two distinct forms of any language, *written* and *spoken*. Teachers of English will insist that syllabication occur after consonant letters in most words of more than one syllable. The word, "planet," for example, must be shown thus: "plan – et." However when one actually *speaks* the word, it becomes "pla – net," doesn't it? This is quite marvelous actually, for it gives us yet another choice for mixing up the *Keyword*. Choose therefore, to break syllables according to the *"written"* model, or the *"spoken"* model. Then <u>stick</u> <u>with it</u>. Don't change back and forth with indecision, for in the end you'll forget which path you took. Select your favorite method, and *freeze your decision!*

Now we'll perform the *third* manipulation, *Case*. There are two easy choices for this:

1. All *UPPERCASE (Capital Letters,)* OR
2. All *lowercase (Small Letters)*

You will select *one* of the two choices for your third *Keyword* manipulation. For this lesson, I'm going to select #2, all *lowercase;*

flogtrac.

WHY?

Good passwords include both uppercase and lowercase letters. However, it is far simpler to be able to choose which letters shall be one or the other while you are creating an actual password. Therefore, your Keyword should be *all* one or the other, providing a generic base from which to deviate as you choose. (More on this in later chapters...)

Before going on to the **Long Phrase** method, we'll do one more of the Short Phrase type because the *No Repeating Characters* rule can often get sticky. Happily, it is easily unstuck.

"golf cart" is what I would call a *logical phrase*. It makes sense, we know what it is and it's a common term. One is not limited to the logical however, and an *illogical* phrase is perfectly acceptable. For example, two words not commonly associated with each other that may produce a somewhat silly phrase might be, "blue garbage." Try as you may, it is unlikely that "blue garbage" should come to mind as a phrase even remotely associated with just about anyone.

It does have repeating characters however, making it ideal for this example. Here you will learn how to get creative with your *Keyword*.

First, we'll do manipulation #1, Sequence Inversion: *bluegarbage* becomes *egabrageulb,* (currently unpronounceable, yes – and fear not, read on.)

Appearing more than once are "e" "g" "a" and "b." So here we shall insert an additional manipulation step I call, "Select and Substitute."

Select:

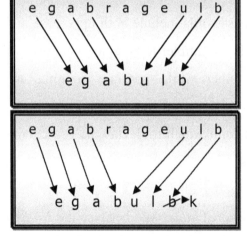

Substitute:

I simply began at the beginning and selected a sequence of letters that would form a *pronounceable* word, preferably with no repeating characters, or at least a minimum. And at the end, I substituted a "k" for the second (repeating) "b" as it just sounded good to me. (You might have chosen another letter.) Now I've ended up with a useable sequence, "egabulk." I may now move on to Manipulation #2, the optional *syllable inversion.* (Remember, I prefer the *spoken* version of syllabication.)

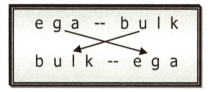

This would give me "bulkega," and I rather like that.

The third manipulation is Case, and I'll use choice #2, all *lowercase.*

Now that I've completed my manipulations, I have bulkega - a *Keyword* that follows all three rules:

1. 2 or 3 syllables of nonsense
2. No repeating characters
3. Pronounceable and Memorizable.

REVIEW:

1. I pulled an *illogical phrase* out of my hat, "blue garbage."

2. After *inverting* the sequence, I selected certain letters out of it to create a *pronounceable* word with a *minimum of* or *no repeating characters.*

3. I *substituted* an unused letter from the alphabet for the final character (because it was a repeater,) and formed a word with a pronunciation I liked.

4. I finished with Manipulations 2 and 3, and created a *Keyword*.

Further: You have learned

1. The use of either a *logical* or an *illogical phrase*

2. How to select certain characters from the original sequence and drop others

3. How to deal with repeating characters

4. How much flexibility one actually has in creating a *Keyword* (quite a bit!)

Think of this; does **flogtrac** bear any resemblance to the phrase from which it was born, "Golf Cart?" That is, if one were to use the word **flogtrac** in conversation, would any listener trace it back to its origin? Doubtful.

And what of **bulkega**? To the uninformed listener, do you think "blue garbage" would ever come to mind?

We've taken two short phrases, one *logical* and one *illogical*, and built two wonderful nonsense words that may be used as *Keywords* in a personal *Alain Code Password System*. (Remember however, *never* to use any of the examples in this book for your own personal *Alain Code*!)

D: Exercise

Now it's your turn. Using your own notebook, take the inverted "blue garbage," that is "egabrageulb," and create two or three possible Keywords from it, using all you've learned thus far. When you've finished, look in **Appendix A, Chapter Two, Exercise 1** (on page 77) to see three possible *Keywords* that I pulled from the same sequence. Yours may be quite different from mine, and that's just fine. Remember, there are no wrong answers as long as your Keywords conform to the three rules:

1. 2 or 3 syllables of nonsense
2. No repeating characters
3. Pronounceable and memorizable

Do the exercise above, then we'll move ahead to the **Long Phrase** method (merely an extension of what you've just learned.)

And do understand that the simple exercises I'll ask you to perform take very little time, and are crucial to the learning process. In order to move ahead, it is essential that you have personally taken pen to paper and experienced the work thus far, step by step.

DO THE EXERCISE BEFORE CONTINUING

E: LONG PHRASE METHOD

The only difference between the *Short* and *Long Phrase* Methods is that the *Long* provides us with more choices for selecting our sequence of letters for a *Keyword*. Where the *Short Phrase* was two words, the *Long Phrase* might be three or four. (More than four isn't necessary.)

Again, an <u>illogical</u> phrase is probably best, as you wouldn't want someone to guess it through its association with you. "Bathe the butterfly," is silly and unlikely to be guessed by even an intimate friend. How about, "Exonerate the shoelace?" All we want really, is a grouping of letters from which we can select a *nonsense, pronounceable sequence*. Right. Let's begin with "Mow the driveway."

Manipulation #1 – Sequence Inversion

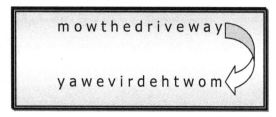

"m o w t h e d r i v e w a y" becomes "y a w e v i r d e h t w o m"

There's quite a bit to work with here, isn't there? Just begin on the left, and select some letters that form something both nonsensical and pronounceable.

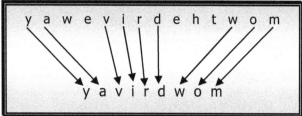

This is my first construct. It's not particularly fun, so I'll drop the "om" at the end and substitute an "e" …

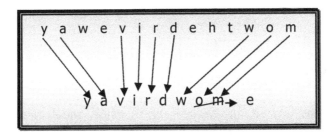

y a v i r d w e

This is better. I substituted the "we" for the "wom," because of pronunciation. Let me explain. Depending upon one's pronunciation of "wom," one might forget it's spelled with an "o" and mistakenly throw in an "a" instead. An American speaker might pronounce it, "wahm," while a European might say, "wawm." Therefore, to avoid a spelling mishap brought about by an ambiguous pronunciation, it is preferable to use spellings that produce only specific sounds. "yavirdwe" might sound like "yah – veerd – wee." However, one might also pronounce the second syllable as "verd" rather than "veerd," thus thinking that it is spelled "verd" not "vird." So I shall simply substitute an "o" for the "i" and my new sequence is, "yavordwe."

Still a bit cumbersome, so let us option Manipulation #2 and rearrange the syllables. We could have "we – ya – vord," or possibly "vord – ya – we," or "vord – we – ya." Personally, and this is just my choice, "we – ya – vord" rolls off my tongue more pleasingly than the others, making it easier for me to memorize. Your opinion may be different, and that's splendid! Your tongue must decide what's best for it, not mine.

Alain deGlanville

Then move on to Manipulation #3, Case, and that's it. You see, all we've done by using the *Long Phrase* method is to have given ourselves many more characters from which to choose for the construction of the *Keyword*.

And once again we've seen just how much license we have to be creative. Each time we *manipulate* our *Keyword*, it becomes more nonsensical, more unrecognizable, and more *suitable*. (And consider: The more *nonsensical* the word is, the *easier* it will be to remember!)

Substitution allows you to eliminate repeating characters, *and* make it more *pronounceable* for you.

F: ASSIGNMENT

Alright, this is it. It's time for you to create your own personal *Keyword* that you shall keep for many years. Experiment with both the *Short Phrase* and *Long Phrase* methods and discover what happens. Come up with two or three choices, then select the best one.

Caution! There is a danger in creating *too many* choices. You may like more than one of them and forget which you've chosen. In particular, if you find yourself vacillating between a couple of choices, that indecision may be your downfall. Therefore I recommend the following procedure:

    1. Begin with either method and create a single *Keyword*.

2. Using either method, create a second *Keyword*.

3. If either of these first two choices feels good and doesn't violate any of the three rules for Keywords, STOP! Pick it. That's your *Keyword!* However, if neither choice excites you, create another one.

4. The moment a *Keyword* feels good to you, **STOP**. That's it. As long as it follows the three rules you have your personal *Keyword*! Too many choices lead to confusion down the road, so keep it simple to preserve your sanity.

5. Congratulations! You have a *Keyword!* Write it down on an index card and put it in a <u>temporary</u> <u>safe</u> <u>place</u>. (Later, you'll transfer it to a truly safe location.)

Alain deGlanville

Chapter Three

STEP ONE: Create Your KEYS; *Keynumber*

(Your KEYS to Success...)

Section A: Keynumber

The Keynumber is made up of one, two-digit number, and one three-digit number, with no repeating digits. We have at our disposal the digits 0 – 9, and we'll use only five of them. Again, we'll want to call up numbers that no person, close to you

> ### *Keynumber:*
>
> *A "random" numerical sequence of five digits to be used in the constructing of Passwords.*

or otherwise, might guess were associated with you in any way. And yes, this'll be as easy as *1 – 2 – 3*.

Here's how to do it:

1. **Randomly Select** one, 2- digit number, and one, three-digit number out of thin air.

    a. Let's say I came up with "18 and 281."

    b. Examine the choices for problems

        i. Right off the bat, 8 is repeated, so I'll drop one of those

ii.   The "1" is also repeated, so that has to go.

c. In fact, I'm just going to repeat #1 above and pull all new numbers: "13" and "807."

d. Re-examine for problems – none found. Good.

2. **Offset** the digits: Is anything really "random?" Consider this – you may believe that you thought up these numbers out of the clear blue sky, but the very fact that they came from within the dark recesses of your mind suggests some deeply hidden significance to you somehow, somewhere. The solution is to change the numbers, but to do so systematically. Therefore, we'll *offset* them. We are beginning with [13, 807]

> ### Offset:
>
> *The linear shift of a given Position or Location by a specified number of spaces either to the left or to the right.*

a. Add all the individual digits together, and continue until you end up with a *single* digit:

  i.   [13807] $1 + 3 + 8 + 0 + 7 = 19$

  ii.   [19] $1 + 9 = 10$

  iii.   [10] $1 + 0 = 1$

b. Now add the "1" to each digit:

  i. $1 + 1 = 2$

  ii. $3 + 1 = 4$

iii.   8 + 1 = 9

iv.   0 + 1 = 1

v.   7 + 1 = 8

vi.   [24918]   is   our   new   (offset) Keynumber.

3. **Invert** the Sequence and **Rearrange** for Pronunciation

a. [24918] becomes [81942] when *inverted.*

b. Speak the sequence aloud: [81-942] = "eighty-one, nine-forty-two" (in *words.*) For me, this is pretty easy to say and memorize, so I'd probably keep [81942].

The three Steps were:

1. **Random Number Selection**

2. **Offset**

3. **Invert and Rearrange.**

Now memorize it. Imagine it's a combination to a safe, and simply memorize the sequence, breaking the number into 2 Segments ("eighty-one, nine-forty-two"). This makes it easier than trying to remember "eight, one, nine, four, two."

Do you see what we've done here? We began with what were seemingly "random" numbers out of my head, and then *offset* and *inverted* them so that they no longer bore any resemblance to the original numbers. And remember that this is because if someone were to ask you to pick any number at random, chances are you'd select a number with some deeply rooted significance to your subconscious, which therefore could be discovered by someone particularly clever. It wouldn't be truly "random." So by going through the above steps, we've sufficiently changed the original numbers that their significance to your secret past has been eliminated – or at least reduced to a minimum.

B: ASSIGNMENT

Your turn now. Using your notebook, create your own personal *Keynumber*, and memorize it. When you've finished, write it down on that same index card where you've written your *Keyword*, and replace it in your temporary "safe" location. After that, you may CONTINUE ON.

> **DO THE EXERCISE BEFORE CONTINUING**

Done?

Do you now have your own personal **Keyword** and **Keynumber**? Super! You've successfully completed the most difficult part of your work, **Step One**.

Congratulations!

Creating and learning your **Keys** takes the most time and effort, and *you've done it*. The rest is painless, and the remaining lessons promise to be fascinating for anyone who played with *secret codes* as a child!

Write your new *Keynumber* on that same index card where you wrote your *Keyword*, and replace it in that temporary safe location.

Take a break if you'd like, or just move on to the next chapter and *Step Two*.

Alain deGlanville

Chapter Four

STEP TWO: Build Your Passwords

(From Sense to Nonsense...)

> **STOP!** DEAR READER, IF YOU HAVEN'T COMPLETED ALL THE
> EXERCISES AND ASSIGNMENTS IN CHAPTERS TWO AND THREE,
> IT IS IMPERATIVE YOU DO SO NOW, BEFORE PROCEEDING!
> DONE? RIGHT THEN. CONTINUE ON...

YOUR *KEYS* UNLOCK EVERYTHING from this point on. Therefore it is vital that you protect them from discovery. You'll want to keep that secret index card handy for a while as we build your list of actual passwords, but as soon as you've completed the lessons in this book, place that card into your own personal safe deposit box or vault, out of the reach of others until your eventual demise.

For these lessons, I shall use the following Keys:

[worbesu] and **[53891]**

(You may wonder why I came up with these keys, rather than any of the others created earlier. You see, while you were doing your exercises I was playing a bit to pass the time – and suddenly, there they were!)

Using this *Keyword* and *Keynumber*, we are about to create some actual Passwords.

Start a new page in your personal notebook, and let's make a list of possible accounts in need of passwords. They might include:

1. Logon to your Internet Service Provider
2. Online banking logon
3. Customer logons at your favorite online shopping sites
4. Online auction account logon
5. Logon at work
6. Computer Logon

Everyone's list is different, so we needn't try to anticipate every possible application. To keep it simple, let's assume only four accounts for these lessons, and make a list of them like this:

Diagram 4-1

ACCOUNT	PASSWORD
Internet Service Provider	
Online Banking	
Auction Account	
Computer Logon	

I might choose to use a very simple Password for my Computer Logon, and that might be my *Keyword* as is [worbesu]. For the others, I'll scramble it up and even insert some numbers from my *Keynumber*. For example: I'll begin with "es" then add "38"

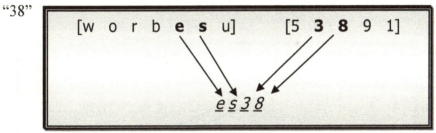

Then I'll add "worb" in one chunk (3 "segments" total.)

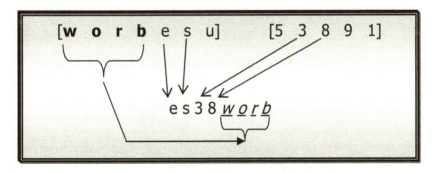

Or, Start with the "w" then bring down "89."

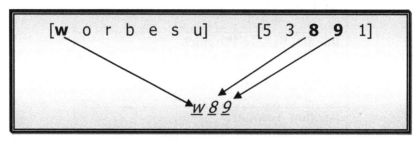

Follow that with the "be."

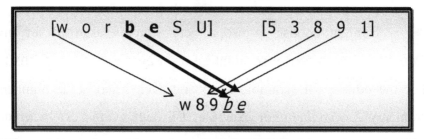

Now we add the "rb" (for a total of 4 "segments.")

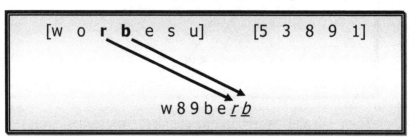

And we have *another* Password, this one with *four* segments! (In a Password, we *are allowed repeating characters!*)

And so on.

(While you weren't looking, I created a third Password. Along with my Keyword as a Password for my Computer Logon, I now have four.) And here is how I would initially note my passwords in my list:

Password Magic

Diagram 4-2

ACCOUNT	PASSWORD
Internet Service Provider	es38worb
Online Banking	w89berb
Auction Account	u91esu
Computer Logon	worbesu

Let's stop here for a moment and cover two matters of import. First and foremost, this written list of passwords is scheduled for destruction by *The Cross-Cut Shredder*! Once you've completed the **Step Three** lessons, you shall recreate this list with *Encoding*, rather than the actual Passwords, and *destroy this first list*.

Second, notice that most of the Passwords are difficult to pronounce. They are total *nonsense-and-scrambled eggs*, and that's the point. No one using only their brains, and even an intimate knowledge of you, should be able to deduce your Passwords.

But what about *you*? If you're going to destroy this list, how shall *you* remember them? Ah, yes. ***Step Three – The Encoding***! It's the little secret that makes it all work – a way of actually making a list of your Passwords that you, and you alone shall be able to read. In fact, *even others who have learned The Alain Code System shall be unable to decipher your Password list,* for without your *KEYS* the

31

Alain deGlanville

list is gibberish! Yes, they'll understand the *system* you've used, but without your *Keys* they'll be unable to unlock a thing.

Right then. Go to your notebook, and using your *Keyword* and your *Keynumber*, create a list of Passwords for three or four of your accounts. (Later, you may go back to your list and complete it. Just do three or four for now.)

Caution: Notice that in my sample list in Diagram 4-2 above, I've created Passwords with only three or four *Segments*. That is, I've taken only three or four *pieces,* or *contiguous character groupings* of my Keyword and Keynumber and strung them together.

When I selected the "be" from my Keyword to be used in the Password "w89berb," the "be" became a *segment.* In fact, it became the *third segment* of the password. The more *pieces* or *segments* I use, the more complex the encoding – and the more difficult to figure out when I go to use it. The current wisdom is that if a Password is made up of 6 to 8 characters of nonsense, it's an extremely good Password. So really, don't get carried away. If the system is too difficult to use easily, you'll stop using it and revert to your old bad habits, won't you? My whole purpose in creating the *Alain Code System* was to make the management of my list of highly secure Passwords *easy*! Do the same for yourself – make it easy!

Another Caution! Ultimately you may wish to use a table in your Word Processor or a Spreadsheet application to maintain your lists (as I have done above.) You've probably noticed when typing on your computer, depending upon which typeface you've chosen, that there could be some confusion in the distinction between certain characters. In the *Times New Roman*[1] typeface for example, the difference between the uppercase "I" (*eye*) and lower case "l" (*el*) is only slight. And the lower case "l" (*el*) and numeral "1" (*one*) are identical. In the *Arial*[2] typeface, uppercase "I" (*eye*) and lower case "l" (*el*) are identical, while the numeral "1" (*one*) is quite distinct.

Notice also "O" and "0." The letter *oh* and numeral *zero*, while different enough, can still be confused if not seen next to each other. Typically, the *oh* will be rounder, fatter [O], and the *zero* more narrow [0].

The point is this – the use of these characters in your Keyword and Keynumber could lead to trouble when encoded, unless one's very careful with the choice of typeface. I've selected three typefaces as examples below.

Diagram 4-3

Typeface	**"Zero"**	**"Oh"**	**"Eye"**	**"El"**	**"One"**
Tahoma[3]	0	O	I	l	1
Garamond[4]	0	O	I	l	1
Verdana[5]	0	O	I	l	1

Alain deGlanville

Of these, I'd select *Tahoma* or *Verdana*. (*Tahoma* is common with Windows® operating systems, while *Verdana* should be available to Mac® users.)

Now go ahead and create your first list of three or four Passwords. When you've done it, proceed to Chapter Five.

Password Magic

Alain deGlanville

Chapter Five

Encoding Primer

(Let's Start With Something Fun!)

IMAGINE THIS: I instruct you to take the word "brown," and beginning with the letter "o" fill a total of 3 spaces – you'd write "own," wouldn't you?

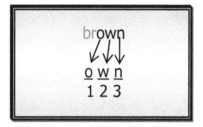

Or if I instructed you to begin with "b" and fill a total of 4 spaces, you'd write "brow."

And finally, imagine that I instructed you to begin with "w" and fill 4 spaces. There are only 2 spaces left in the word, but you're intelligent so you circle back to the

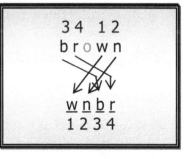

beginning of the word to finish, and come up with "wnbr."

Alain deGlanville

The above examples have introduced you to one of the core principals of the *Alain Code System* – that the CODE itself is merely a set of *instructions* for recreating your Passwords!

Let's face it. If one were allowed to write one's passwords down on paper and carry them around, coming up with some truly unbreakable sequences of nonsense (great passwords,) wouldn't be a problem.

One would be able to follow all the rules such as, "Use a different password for each account," and "Don't use the name of one's pet parakeet," etc. Except that there's that other, most important rule: "Never write passwords down anywhere!"

It's a Dilemma!

In Chapter One I said that I've broken the *Alain Code System* into three steps.

1. **Forge Your Keys**
2. **Create Your Passwords**
3. **Lock Your Passwords (*Encoding*)**

Number *three* is what makes it all possible. So here in Chapter Five, I'm going to give you a quick lesson in the Encoding process (Step Three) as a sort of *Encoding Primer* or *Introduction To Encoding*, which will be covered in Chapter Six.

You'll learn that one actually can make a list of all one's passwords that no one else may figure out – even someone who has read this book! Fair enough?

And the best news of all – it's as easy as "1 – 2 – 3!"

You've now created your own personal *Keys,* and some Passwords for yourself. And to keep things simple, for the purposes of this lesson I'll use only a *Keyword,* and that shall be "belfast."

Now this would be a most *in*appropriate *Key,* as it is the name of a city in a country to which some of my ancestors have ties. It's a common word, has a definition, and could be deduced by someone who knew me well enough. Very Bad Key! And *perfect* for this lesson, actually.

Even though we may create many passwords out of this one *Key,* we'll start with the simplest one, and that would be to use the *Key* itself as a password.

I've decided to use it for the Password to my email account. The encoding for this one is quite simple:

[b7]

Can you figure out what that means? A CODE Segment has two "positions" in it, #1 and #2. Position #1 contains the Beginning Character, and #2 contains the Length of that Segment in the actual Password.

> ### *Length:*
>
> *The total number of Characters in a Password Segment*

[b7] tells me to take my *Keyword*, begin with the letter "b" and continue for a *total Length* of seven consecutive Characters. It's too simple, isn't it? [b7] = [belfast].

All right then, let's go a bit further. Suppose I decide to use five of the middle letters for my online auction account.

> ### *Code:*
>
> *The encoded instruction-set for recreating any given Password*

"elfas"

You already know what the CODE will be for this, don't you?

[e5]

Begin with the "e" in my *Keyword* and continue for the next four Spaces, for a *total Length* of *five* consecutive letters.

Shall we get really tricky? Let's take the last two letters and the first two and put together "**stbe**" as a password.

In the previous examples, I selected one unbroken sequence

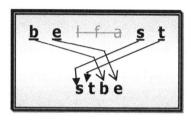

of letters for each password, so the encoding needed only one *Segment*. This is the case also with "**stbe**," as I started with the "**s**" and continued for a total of *four consecutive Characters.*

(If the number of spaces takes me past the end of the *Keyword*, I simply go back to the beginning.)

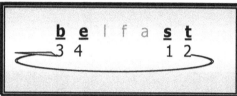

The CODE is [**s**4] of course.

This time I'll begin with a code, and you must figure out the password. (This one is even trickier...)

[b2.s2.]

Segment:

In a Password: A consecutive sequence of characters taken from either a Keyword or a Key Number. In a CODE: A two-Character sequence that serves as an "instruction-set" for the construction of the referred Password Segment.

This CODE has two *Segments*, meaning that there are *two* Character Sequences put together. It means:

Alain deGlanville

Begin with the "**b**" for a total Length of *two consecutive Characters* "**be**", then begin with the "**s**" for a total of *two consecutive Characters* "**st**". Put them together for, "**best**."

[b2.s2]

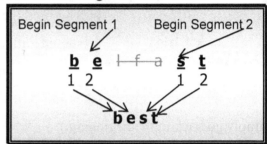

Notice that I've used a *separator* between the CODE Segments – in this case a *period* [.]. After you've learned the system,

Separator:

A symbol, sometimes a punctuation symbol, that does not occur in the KEYS, used to separate each CODE Segment from other Segments

you'll learn of alternatives to this, designed to confuse the onlooker. For these lessons however, let's keep it simple and use the period.

We now have four passwords made from the single *Keyword*, and one might write them down in a chart something like this:

ACCOUNT	CODE
Email	b7
Auction	e5
Bank	s4
ISP	b2.s2

As long as no one knows, or can figure out your *Keyword*, they won't have a clue as to what the CODEs mean. One may have a list of dozens of passwords constructed from the same *Keyword* (*not* this *Keyword, but a* real *one*,) and keep a list like this that anyone may view in blissful ignorance!

Of course I've used a very bad *Keyword* here, thus all the Passwords constructed from it are useless. Don't fret though – writing excellent Passwords is as easy as *1 – 2 – 3*, as you've seen.

In summary, the *Code* is nothing more than a ***set of instructions*** for the reconstruction of your Password. It's that simple.

Segment by *segment*, the instructions tell you which character in your *Key* is the *Beginning Character* in that *segment*, and how many of the following characters to use in that same *segment,* to equal the *total length* indicated.

And as you **practice**, it becomes surprisingly second-nature!

Alright, on to Chapter SIX and the real *Encoding* lessons.

Alain deGlanville

Chapter Six

STEP THREE: Encode Your List

(From Nonsense to Sense...)

Now that you've begun a list of Passwords for some of your accounts, you have what you'll need to perfect your skills at Encoding. In Chapter Five I introduced you to the Encoding process on a very basic level. Now we'll get slightly more detailed, even though it remains simple and easy. Once you understand the concept, applying it will become second nature.

Do you remember in Chapter Five I used "belfast" as a Keyword? And as an example, I selected the "be" from the beginning of the word and the "st" from the end and put them together as one of the sample Passwords, "best." It's a

---

Segment:

In a Password: A consecutive sequence of characters taken from either a Keyword or a Keynumber. In a CODE: A two-Character sequence that serves as an "instruction-set" for the construction of the referred Password Segment.

Password with *two Segments*, and the CODE was [b2.s2].

You'll recall that the *encoding*, which is nothing more than a *set of instructions*, told me to begin with the "b" and continue for a *total of 2* consecutive characters ("be") and then begin again with the "s" and continue for a *total of 2* consecutive characters as well ("st") then put them together — "best."

The *encoding* utilizes Segments containing two characters each. The character in Position #1 tells us the *Beginning Character* in that Segment of the Password, and the character in Position #2 tells us the *total number of consecutive characters* in that Segment.

Position:

A given Character's place within a Sequence of Characters.

Thus [b2] instructs us that our Beginning Character is the "b," and that the Segment has a *total of 2* characters in it. From the Keyword "belfast," that would be "be."

The first CODE Segment is followed by a period to separate it from the next one, and we can see that this particular Password has *two Segments* to it, "be" and "st" (The CODE for "st" is [s2].)

For the Encoding to work, you must know your Keys. It's that simple. Now let's encode our sample list of Passwords from Chapter Four. *Do this in your notebook along with me*. We'll start with the Password "es38worb".

Your KEYs are: [worbesu] and [53891]

1. Begin with the "e" and continue for a total of 2 consecutive characters "es" ╱*Beginning Character*

    a. The CODE is [e2] ←*Segment Length*

2. As the next character is a number, we know we've now gone to the Key*number*. Begin with the "3" and continue for a total of 2 consecutive characters to get "38"

    a. [32] is the CODE segment

3. Back to the Key*word* now, and start with the "w" and continue for a total of 4 consecutive characters to get "worb."

    a. [w4] is the CODE segment

Putting the three Segments of the code together, separating each segment with a period, looks like this: [e2.32.w4]

Did you get the same answer in your notebook?

A word about CASE...

Passwords are *case-sensitive*. That means that in creating a password, if you choose to include an uppercase B in it, then you must always enter that password with that same uppercase B, or you'll get an error-message. (And as good passwords contain both *upper*case <u>and</u> *lower*case letters, we'll cover that option in Chapter 8.)

Now let us *de*construct the code to test it (*decoding.*) *Do this in your notebook along with me also.*

Alain deGlanville

Your KEYs are: [worbesu] and [53891] and the CODE is [e2.32.w4]

1. [e2] Begin with the "e" for a total of 2 characters
   a. "es"
2. [32] Begin with the "3" for a total of 2 characters
   a. "38"
3. [w4] Begin with the "w" for a total of 4 characters
   a. "worb"
4. String it all together:
   a. "es" & "38" & "worb" = "es38worb"
   b. The CODE is [e2.32.w4]
   c. The Password is [es38worb]

Using it is quite simple. Imagine you're on line and about to enter a password. You consult your encoded list, select the appropriate account, and following your CODE (*instructions*) with your memorized KEYS you simply enter the indicated characters and off you go!

> YOUR **CODE** is merely a set of step-by-step instructions on what to key in!

Now here's another warning about getting too complicated. If you think about it, the process of creating your KEYS was so multi-layered that your Keys alone would make excellent Passwords.

48

I suggest you use them, or extremely simple constructs from them for your most oft used accounts. You'll quickly find that you've learned even these Passwords and won't need your Encoded List.

Surely by now my constant harping about keeping it *simple and easy* should be getting through to you. Your therapist is wealthy enough, so ***keep it simple!***

Now it's your turn again. On the next page is the list I created in Chapter 4. In your notebook, *encode* the remaining Passwords. THEN- Test your work by <u>DE</u>coding, and confirming your accuracy. *This is a most important step*!

AFTER ENCODING a Password, always do a *Test Decoding* to confirm the accuracy of your CODE.

After checking your work, compare your answers to mine by turning to Appendix A, Chapter Six, Exercise One (found on page 77.)

KEYs: [**worbesu**] and [**53891**]

Alain deGlanville

Diagram 6-1

ACCOUNT	*PASSWORD*	*ENCODING*
Internet Service Provider	es38worb	e2.32.w4
Online Banking	w89berb	
Auction Account	u91esu	
Computer Logon	worbesu	

DO THE EXERCISE BEFORE CONTINUING

Got the hang of it? Super. Go back to your notebook now, to your own list of personal Passwords and ENCODE them! And don't forget to DECODE as well, to check your accuracy. Do that, *then* return to this lesson.

DO THE EXERCISE BEFORE CONTINUING

Finished? Right.

You are now ready to create your *list document*. This is as easy as opening your favorite word processor and inserting a "table" on the page, just as you see in Diagram 6-2, or using your favorite spreadsheet application. Only *your* table shall use the THREE columns, you'll see below, not two. They should be labeled as you see in Diagram 6-2:

Diagram 6-2

ACCOUNT	USERNAME	CODE
(Account Name 1)	*(USERNAME)*	*(ENCODED Password)*
(Account Name 2)	*(USERNAME)*	*(ENCODED Password)*
Etc. ...	*Etc. ...*	*Etc. ...*

Do remember to use an appropriate typeface for your CODEs.

USERNAMEs don't have to be encoded. Typically, they follow certain conventions and are easy to guess anyway. (Jonathan P. Terwilliger's USERNAME will most likely be **johnt**, as assigned by his company's I.T. department, and everyone will know it!) Besides, they're worthless without the *password!*

And the really wonderful thing is that you needn't worry about protecting the document. *AS LONG AS NO ONE KNOWS YOUR KEYS, YOUR ENCODED LIST SHALL BE MEANINGLESS TO ALL BUT YOU.* Thus you may carry it with you, tape it to your desk or monitor in full view of all, keep a copy in your wallet/purse/briefcase/lunch bag- all without worry.

Congratulations!

You've completed the basic lessons; you've learned the *System* and have begun your list of Passwords. You've accomplished an *enormous* amount.

Once you've completed *all* the lessons in this book, place your index card into your vault or bank safe deposit box. You don't want to shred your keys. Illness, accidents and injuries are common causes of memory loss, however short-term, and you certainly wouldn't want your keys to be irretrievably lost to you.

Well done.

In the next chapters, we'll advance to the use of UPPERCASE/lowercase letters, and non-alpha characters (symbols from your keyboard.)

Password Magic

Alain deGlanville

Chapter Seven

Alternative Periods

(Separation Anxiety!)

IN CHAPTER SIX, I used [e2.32.w4] as one of my codes. Using the *period* ".." as a *separator* is simple and probably suitable most of the time. However it does clearly delineate the two-character *segments* of the code, even to the casual onlooker. They'll notice the obvious symmetry, and the more adventuresome among them (your own children, perhaps?) may be sufficiently intrigued to attempt to figure it out.

But what if your code looked like this?

[e2!32xw4]

I used "!" and "x" as *separators*, removing any obvious *segmentation*. Here's the trick. I may use *any* character *not* found in my Keys as a *separator*.

I could use [e2232)w4]. There is no numeral "2" in my Keys, and no *non*-alpha symbols ")". The following are three more examples of the identical code:

[e2A327w4]

[e2*32cw4]

[e2(32!w4]

Alain deGlanville

Look, you know that your code is made up of 2-character *segments*, so the *third* character has to be a *separator*, right?

Any character that is not a *Key character* must be a *separator*. [e2A] would be the same as [e2.].

Now here's an added advantage. While [e2.32.w4] might appear to be a *code*, [e2A32*w4] would rather appear to be the *actual password*. And even though it wouldn't work if some twit should try it, said twit is more likely to think that you've *changed* your password and give up, than realize it's a *code*.

Further confusion can be thrust upon your local nosy nimrods by *adding* characters to the *beginning* and *end* of your code. (Again, use only *non-key* characters.)

[e2A327w4] could become [de2A327w4!]

When *de*-coding, ignore all characters that are not found in your *Keys*, the *non-key* characters. d is not a *key character*, so it is ignored and the *segment* begins with the e. By not *seeing* the *non-key characters* [de2A327w4!], all that's left is e2 32 w4. Twits and nimrods won't know what to ignore, or even that they should!

Now if you'd like, you may return to your list of codes and substitute *non-key* characters for the *periods* we originally used as *separators*.

You've now learned one additional *level* of encryption. Again, practice will make it easy for you, and that much more stupefying for the unauthorized onlooker.

Password Magic

Alain deGlanville

Chapter Eight

The "Shift" CODE

(A Rather Shifty Character...)

IN THIS CHAPTER, we shall focus on *increasing the encryption* level of your Passwords by adding *UPPER* or *LOWER* case letters wherever we choose, and even *symbol characters*, or both.

Earlier, you chose to have your Keyword represented either in all *UPPERCASE* or all *lowercase* letters. (For these lessons, I chose *lowercase.*) Now you'll see how to change the *case* of any letter at will.

Doing this requires no change in your Keys at all. You've created them and learned them, and shall continue to use them. But you'll now know how to change the *case* of any letter in your password. For example, w89berb could become w89**B**erb very easily.

Step One: Select Your *Shift Code Letter*

Method #1: My Keyword contains seven letters, leaving a few unused letters from the original Short Phrase. In creating "worbesu," there were letters within my Short Phrase that I dropped. Some were "repeaters," others were not. There was an "n" and an "h" that were non-repeaters, so they are good choices for my Shift Code Letters.

If you have nothing useable left over from creating your Keyword, use the following process to assure that the letters with which you end up are chosen as randomly as possible.

Method #2:

1. Add together all the individual digits in your Keynumber

    a. My Keynumber is [53891], so
       $5+3+8+9+1 = 26$

2. Then add those two digits together

    a. $2 + 6 = 8$

3. [8] Begin with the first letter in the alphabet that doesn't appear in your Keyword, and count through them – skipping those letters in your Keyword – until you reach (in my case) the 8th one. (Your number is bound to be different, of course.) In the diagrams below, I grayed out the letters in my Keyword, and skipped them as I counted.

a	b	c	d	e	f	g	h	i	j	k	l	m
1		2	3		4	5	6	7	*8*			

4. Now reverse the process. Begin at the END of the alphabet and count to the same number, Right to Left:

_n_	o	p	q	r	s	t	u	v	w	x	y	z
_8_		7	6			5		4		3	2	1

The first count yields a "j" and the second one lands on "n." Now remember, you need do this only once. You will select only ONE letter. I'll use [n] as the Shift Code Letter for the lesson, but you'll need your own for your passwords. Remember, the Shift Code Letter must be one that does *not* appear in your Keyword.

Go ahead and select an alphabet letter to use for your Shift Code Letter, and be sure to use one of the two methods above to assure randomness. Method #1 is preferred of course, so use Method #2 only if you do not have any "non-repeating" letters left over from the building of your Keyword.

Step Two: Select your *Shift Code Number*

All together, you'll have one Shift Code Letter and one Shift Code *Number*. Since your Keynumber contains five of the ten available digits (0-9) there are five remaining. Take the same number you used to find your Shift Code Letter (in my case "8") and count through the remaining digits, returning to the beginning again as necessary, until you reach the 8th one. My remaining digits are "2" "4" "6" "7" and "0":

Alain deGlanville

2	4	6	7	0	2	4	_6_	7	0
1	2	3	4	5	6	7	_8_		

My Shift Code Number shall be [6]. How about you? Go ahead and find your own personal Shift Code Number. (By the way, I could have started just as easily at the end of my numbers and counted from right to left, landing on the "6" again as the 8th digit. Do it either way!)

Got it? Super. Remember, for the lesson we'll be using [n] and [6].

In the Alain Code, each encoding segment contains two character positions. The first character of the CODE identifies the starting character from the Keyword/Keynumber, and the second character of the CODE gives us the number of consecutive spaces in the *overall length* of that segment.

The CODE [w2] would yield "wo" for that Password Segment, correct? (We're still using "worbesu" as our Keyword.)

Remember however, that we may arbitrarily add any non-key character between *segments* as a separator, or even at the very beginning where a separator isn't technically required, disguising the separator and confusing the twits. Substituting a *Shift Code Character* for a *separator* will cause that character to serve as both a separator, and an instruction to *SHIFT* the next character in the Code.

Adding an [n] (our new Shift Code Letter) will change things. The CODE [nw2] tells us to SHIFT (change the case) of the Starting Character. Therefore, rather than getting "wo," we now have "Wo." Since the "w" in the Keyword is *lowercase*, it "shifts" to *UPPER*case. (If your Keyword is all UPPERCASE, then the "shift" would be to *LOWERcase*.)

CODE [ne3] says that the letters will be "esu" from the Keyword, but the Starting Character will "shift" to *uppercase*, "E." The resulting Password Segment would be "Esu."

What about the Shift Code Number? Very good question. They're *interchangeable!*

Snap-Quiz: Decode [682] (Your Keynumber is 53891.)

Hint- the 6 is a Shift Code Character...

Let's figure it out. Did you get "*9" as the decoded password segment?

"82" as a code would produce "89" as that password segment, wouldn't it? Begin with the "8" in the Keynumber and continue for a total segment length of 2 places. 89. And by adding the Shift Code Character "6" ahead of it, the "8" becomes "**Shift-8**" or "*" on my keyboard.

See how that works? By the way, we could have used our other Shift Code Character, "n" instead: "n82". The result would be exactly the same. [*9].

Alain deGlanville

Suppose we planned to use wor89 as a password, and are being prompted to include both Upper and Lower Case letters, *and a symbol*.

The Code for wor89 would be w3.82 in its simplest form, or perhaps w3!82+ in a more misleading form, substituting non-key characters as separators.

Now let's insert one of the Shift Code Characters ahead of the w: nw3!82+. This will change the password from wor89 to Wor89. Shift-w = W.

Using another Shift Code Character before the "8" would produce the "*" in the password: nw3682+ = Wor*9. What if the code were 6w3n82+? (Trick question...) Answer: **They're identical!** Our Shift Code Characters, "6" and "n" are *interchangeable*, and using a numeral before a letter and vice versa makes the code more readable for you. Ready for more?

Wor*9 is a five-character password. Suppose you are being prompted for a six-character password. OK, there are a couple of ways to do this. The simplest might be to change the Code from 6w3n82+ to 6w3n8_3+. (Start with the "8" and fill for a total of 3 places, and be sure to use Shift-8 as the first one: Wor*91 – a six-character password.)

A more fun way to do it, and more confusing for anyone peering at your list, is to use one of the Shift Code Characters as an "INSERT" instruction. Very simply, here is how it works: A Shift Code Character *followed by a non-key character* means to INSERT that character (*shifted*) into the password. This is an INSERTED SEGMENT, of single-character length.

Example: n71 is decoded as follows...

n = INSERT-SHIFT (because "7" is a non-key character.)

7 = & when Shifted

1 = a segment length of one space.

OR: n&1 would decode as... "Shift-"&"", or "7". (If Shift-7 = &, then Shift-& = 7. Simple?

Let's include this little gem in a password. We'll change Wor*9 to Wor*9&:

Code = 6w3n82n71+

6w3 = Wor

n82 = *9

n71 = &

+ = an added separator, and is meaningless.

6w3n82n71+ decodes to Wor*9&.

Thus we have inserted "&" as a whole new segment into the password. This has the added advantage of *inserting* a new *random* element to the CODE – 6w3n82*n71*+. You may insert letters, numbers and symbols, upper- or lowercase. (6N1 = n.) Your CODE appears to be an *actual PASSWORD*, and our local nimrods will face even greater frustrations!

A FLAW IN THE SOUP?

No doubt you have now discovered a potential vulnerability in the Alain Code System. Clever you! Yes, there is; and there is a simple solution!

Others who have read this book will be familiar with the basic structure of the coding- two-character segments beginning with a key letter or number, followed by the segment length. Careful study could lead to the discovery of some, if not all of the characters in your keys. Preventing this is as simple as carefully restricting the characters you are willing to give away, and the systematic inclusion of non-key characters as subterfuge.

RESTRICTING:

1. Use only *consonants (not vowels)* to begin your segments.

    a. There are only 5 (sometimes 6) vowels in our alphabet, so giving away any of the vowels in our Keyword makes guessing the others much easier. With so many consonants from which to choose, guessing is far less likely.

2. Use the *same* 2 or 3 consonants all the time.

    a. The fewer characters you give away, the less likely anyone will be able to guess the others.

3. Select only TWO of your Keynumbers to use as beginning characters.

CONFUSING:

1. Select THREE *NON-KEY LETTERS* (do not use the SHIFT letter,) as "Red Herrings."

2. Select TWO *NON-KEY NUMBERS* as additional "Red Herrings."

As an example, with worbesu and 53891 as our KEYS, I would select w b and s as my constant consonants, and 5 and 9 as my constant numbers. n and 6 are my Shift Characters, so I'll select c k and p, and 2 and 7 as my non-key "Red Herrings." (Just random selections.)

If my password is to be wo53Suw, the basic code would be w2.526s3. (My segments all begin with some of my "constants," w, s and 5.)

Inserting my Red Herrings, the code becomes c3!w2z52ap16s3.

The *phantom* characters in the code are *c3! z ap1*. So in the code, you should see: c3!w2z52ap16s3, or w2 52 6s3.

You now have even those other intrepid and savvy computer users who've read this book thoroughly confused.

As Sheldon might say, "*Bazinga!*"[6]

OK, that's it! You've completed the course, and are ready to use some incredibly secure passwords wherever you choose.

Congratulations. You're *brilliant!*

Alain deGlanville

Chapter Nine

SECURITY – Your Responsibility

(Looking Out for Number-One!)

NOW THAT YOU'VE SOLVED all of your nasty *Password Problems*, let's take a quick look at perhaps your greatest security vulnerability: The INTERNET!

Every computer user should have the latest anti-virus software installed, with an active account with its publisher to assure the latest virus definition updates. The best applications will protect you from malicious websites, will scan your email as it downloads and remove infected attachments, and generally protect you from the most common threats out there.

However, *nothing's 100%!* You must do your part as well. Cyber-vandals and cyber-criminals are constantly looking for the chinks in our armor; a way in to our most private information, or just to wipe out our files and destroy years of work. They may be after our identity, or they may simply want to send emails to everyone in our address book, using our email address as the "return" or "Reply-To" address so that the recipients think it's coming from us and will trust it.

A few simple rules and guidelines can save you from a world of heartache or financial woes. You've probably heard most of this before, yet it bears repeating.

Alain deGlanville

EMAIL is the most common vehicle for spyware, viruses and phishers. These emails use *links* and *attachments*, and are *unsolicited* (meaning you weren't expecting them, or did not request them.) Sometimes they will

> ### *phishing:*
>
> *Tricking unwary users into divulging logon, password, pin, credit card account and other personal information.*

very cleverly appear to be from your bank, or PayPal®, telling you that due to a security breach, or new security procedures, you are to click on a link to go to their website and renew your password or PIN, etc.

DON'T!

An email that says it's from the US Postal Service, or UPS may contain an attachment with delivery information of a parcel that couldn't be delivered, with instructions to open the attachment for details.

DON'T!

The "FBI" may inform you, (using somewhat questionable grammar and sentence structure) that they've confirmed the fact that you've won a lot of money in some lottery... just click here... (etc.)

DON'T!

DON'T!

70

I'm a fairly *literal* person, and folks who throw words like "always," and "never," around like so much cheap confetti, drive me to distraction.

"You *never* give me credit for *anything!*" or "I'm *always* picking up after you…" are exaggerations that compromise credulity. Of course, they *mean*, "sometimes…" but to make their point, they embellish by invoking infinity.

I try my best to follow the simple rule, *Never say "Never."*

I mention this only to prepare you. After much consideration and soul-searching, I find I *must* use the word:

NEVER open an attachment, or click on a link in an *unsolicited* email!

Shall I repeat that, or do you get my drift? Even FURTHER…

Emails from friends and acquaintances actually could have originated from a malicious source, especially if you weren't expecting them, and if they contain attachments or links. The safest thing to do is to CALL the alleged sender on the *telephone*, (yes, the old-fashioned way where two humans actually speak with one another,) and confirm that they did send the email.

The Internet is a fantastic resource. It is exciting, loaded with information and endless entertainment. And *it is dangerous*.

Too many innocent children have been lured into hazardous situations, even death. Unsuspecting adults, meeting someone to pick up or deliver an auctioned item have arrived at a secluded location only to be held up at gunpoint. Credit card numbers, Social Security numbers, mothers' maiden names and tons of other personal information remain the constant targets of criminals with hacking skills.

And honestly, your only protection is your own diligence, and common sense. For your children who, let's face it, *have* no common sense, yours must prevail.

It's like driving a car- if you rely on other drivers to watch out for your safety, you'll die. When you're in the driver's seat, it's all on you.

And when you're surfing the Internet, *you're driving!*

Password Magic

Alain deGlanville

Afterword

A closing thought...

(Music to your ears)

THERE IS AN OLD JOKE about a tourist finding his way around New York City, who asked a fellow on the sidewalk, "How do I get to Carnegie Hall?"

His answer? *"Practice."*

Practice!

How will you get to the point where *The Alain Code* is easy to use on a daily basis?

"Practice."

Bless you all,

Alain deGlanville

Alain deGlanville

Appendix A

Solutions To Exercises

Chapter Two, Exercise 1

    I came up with these three possibilities:

        1. bragulp

        2. egabruk

        3. ulbegar

Chapter Six, Exercise One

ACCOUNT	*PASSWORD*	*ENCODING*
Internet Service Provider	es38worb	e2.32.w4
Online Banking	w89berb	w1.82.b2.r2
Auction Account	u91esu	u1.92.e3
Computer Login	worbesu	w7

Alain deGlanville

Footnotes

1: *Times New Roman (Open Type) Version 3.00; Typeface © The Monotype Corporation plc. Data © The Monotype Corporation plc/Type Solutions Inc. 1990-1992. All Rights Reserved*

2: *Arial (Open Face) Version 3.00; Typeface © The Monotype Corporation plc. Data © The Monotype Corporation plc/Type Solutions Inc. 1990-1992. All Rights Reserved*

3: *Tahoma (Open Face) Version 3.14; © 2004 Microsoft Corporation. All Rights Reserved*

4: *Garamond (Open Face)Version 2.35;Digitized data copyright Monotype Lithography, Ltd 1991-1995. All Rights Reserved. Monotype Garamond® is a trademark of Monotype Typography, Ltd which may be registered in certain jurisdictions.*

5: *Verdana (Open Face) Version 2.43; Typeface and data © 1996 Microsoft Corporation. All Rights Reserved*

6: *"Bazinga:" A favorite "gotcha…" expression of Dr. Sheldon Cooper, a lead character in the TV sitcom, "The Big Bang Theory," played by actor Jim Parsons; Chuck Lorre and Bill Prady, Creators; Chuck Lorre, Executive Producer.*